The

Best

School

Practical Ideas on What *Really* Works in Education

Keen Babbage, Ed. D.

Copyright © 2016 Cherrymoon Media

www.cherrymoonmedia.com

ISBN: 0-9982190-0-2
ISBN-13: 978-0-9982190-0-4

DEDICATION

To all people who work at schools to make their school
the best

CONTENTS

INTRODUCTION

The fundamental idea in this book is that every school can be the best school. The best school is not one unique, solitary, isolated academic oasis which no other school can equal. The best school is not the result of a competition or a ranking.

The best school is the product of a way of thinking, of leading, of managing, of teaching, of working, and of decision making that results in attaining bestness, or if you prefer, best-ness. What is bestness? It is the quality of being the true best.

Is your school the best that it has ever been? If yes, that is important, but it may not be sufficient. Is your school best that a school can be? Is your school doing everything that is the absolute best for students, teachers, staff, and administrators? Is your school doing the best for taxpayers?

Has your school removed everything that is a barrier to, a limit to, harmful to, or a reduction of bestness? Has your school increased or added everything needed to cause bestness?

Does your school filter every decision and every

action through this question: does this cause us to be the best school which completely fulfills our school purpose?

A school can be a place where things just happen and school is the sum of what all people at the school do day after day. That is unacceptable because it is a school without direction, without meaning, and without harmonious pursuit of complete achievement of the school's purpose. Unless every person at school and every action at school move in the same direction, the school can be limited to wandering aimlessly.

This book is based on 40 years of seriously active research, study, experience, work and thought. During the years 1976-2016, I worked full-time, with 32 of those career years in education and eight of those career years in advertising/marketing.

In 2016 I retired from public education. A suggestion was made that after retirement I could write a "tell all" book about education. The suggestion did not mean to create sensationalized revelations or "gotcha" episodes. Rather, the idea was understood to "tell all that matters," meaning to be practical, realistic, and authentic. The idea was to provide a voice for the view of school from the most important perspectives: the view seen only from the classroom in particular and from the school itself overall.

This book will "tell all" in that these pages express lessons learned from working in five different schools in addition to working in three large companies. This book also borrows from lessons learned during my education, especially in graduate school when I earned a doctorate in education. The ideas in this book come from overall insights learned from 40 years of work and are not based on any one place or on the actions of any individual person. Specific situations presented in the book are fictional, but ideas and topics presented in the book are very genuine.

This book is written with a certainty, a conviction, a confirmed conclusion that we know what works in education. The truth also is that we know what does not work in education. Reaching a school's purpose by doing what works best and what matters most can be done if what works best and what matters most govern actions and decisions; however, quite unacceptably that does not always happen.

The best school concentrates on doing what works best and on doing what matters most. What is done at the best school? What is not done at the best school? This book is a journey through and a path for thinking about those questions and related topics.

The reader is asked to interact vibrantly with this book. Please do not read this book passively; rather, read this book with an intellectual activity level that analyzes, explores, ponders, questions, agrees, disagrees, creates, and soars.

As you read this book, please respond in your mind to the ideas which you encounter. The journey toward bestness, the attainment of bestness, and the continuation of being the best school will require the involvement and dedication of many people.

This short book is not a tome which specifically addresses every issue, concern, problem, law, policy, regulation, or process related to education. Yet, this book does present an effective way of and basis for thinking about school and of taking actions that can be applied to the wide range of education issues. This book concisely, precisely, and efficiently concentrates on what matters most and on what works best. This approach liberates thought and action to concentrate on what is vital. This avoids getting trapped in micro-management minutiae or in a bureaucratic vortex.

Truth emerges when ideas collide. This book is designed to be a catalyst for the identification of, the creation of, and the productive collision of ideas which, upon clarification followed by complete and continuing implementation, can produce the best school. This book is not a formula or a set of prescriptions; rather, this book is a collection of insights, thoughts, concepts, topics, actions and ideas which the reader should think about and then identify specific actions which would help the school or schools of concern to the reader become the best, one school at a time.

The title of this book, *The Best School*, uses the singular form of school intentionally. Each school can reach the level of the best school. That bestness level can be reached by each school individually. The best school level is not reached across multiple schools simultaneously impacted by the newest effort of the education hierarchy to radically, quickly, autocratically, and bureaucratically transform many schools or all schools with the latest top-down mandated reform of education. Such efforts, usually seasoned with good intentions, have much better intentions than they have results.

The best school is not powered by intentions. The best school is powered by sensible, practical, ethical, honorable actions that get the desired results. Each school can get great results. Each school can reach bestness. Let's think about how to make that happen.

Keen Babbage
Lexington, Kentucky
November 2016

REALITY: NOT THEORY, NOT PHILOSOPHY

Consider this unexpected perspective – education has more solutions than it has problems. Unrealistic, unnecessary, disruptive, bureaucratic, so-called solutions are imposed on schools continuously. Many of these mistakes disappear after a few years of doing damage only to be replaced by more, possibly worse, micro-mismanagement invasions of schools and classrooms.

What causes these sophisticated, elaborate, intricate, imitative solutions to fail? They fail because they are not based on school reality and on classroom reality. How can school reality and classroom reality be known? Experience the reality fully; listen thoroughly and often to people who experience the reality daily; or do both which is the superior option.

Some, perhaps many, innovations, educational experiments, reforms or other trial and error actions which are imposed on schools and classrooms are very temporary trends which arouse much publicity and fanfare claiming to be the long-awaited ultimate solution to the problems of education. After failing to solve those problems, the phantom non-solution is discarded and sent to the education reform landfill to join other dismal debacles.

Being the best school begins with and continues with a very accurate and very current understanding of school reality with emphasis on classroom reality. Some people who seek to improve schools do not work at a school. To make their efforts and ideas legitimate, these people must spend much time at schools and must invest much time listening to people who do work at schools. These people could increase their effectiveness by concentrating on schools one at a time rather than on the universe of schools because each school is unique in terms of strengths, weaknesses, successes, failures, achievements, problems, needs, and resources.

School reality and classroom reality include, but are not limited to, the following:

(1) "I spread those rumors because I wanted to see a fight," said the eighth grader to the assistant principal as a hallway brawl was investigated. Reality – instead of concentrating on learning, the eight grader concentrated on manipulating two seventh graders into a fight. The fight happened, injuries occurred, school was disrupted, and no education reformers were there to experience this reality or to offer a solution.

(2) "I found it," was the response of the tenth grader when a school law enforcement officer investigated another cell phone theft. Additional evidence would prove that the tenth grader had stolen the phone. This was the third time during the school year that the same student had stolen a cell phone at school. The student has been absent from school often and is failing all classes. The student has disrupted several classes multiple times during the school year. Social engineers claim the school is insensitive to the needs of the

student. Teachers and the school principal say they have tried every available option to work with the student. Why is theft of a cell phone at school called "a bad choice" instead of a crime, some educators ask.

(3) The student walked into her eleventh grade math class saying to a friend, "I had to work at my job really late last night. I was there until we closed. I'm so tired. I'll sleep through this class. They can't do anything about me sleeping if I decide to sleep." When the teacher told the student to wake up and do the assigned work, the student said for all to hear, "You ain't my daddy. You can't tell me what do."

(4) As the sixth grade math teacher collected homework papers, eight out of 27 students had nothing to turn in. In class the day before, the teacher had made sure that every student began working on the homework during the final 10 minutes of class. She monitored that work time closely and individually to be sure each student began well. Several of those eight students rarely turn in homework despite persistent effort and caring encouragement from the teacher.

(5) As the high school English teacher collected student essays that were assigned one week ago, she heard these comments: "I worked hard on that. I think it's the best paper I have written." "I didn't do the paper. Can I get half credit tomorrow?" "It's finished, but I didn't get it printed. I know it is due, like now, but can I turn it in late?" "You will be impressed with my paper. It's great." The students have been told many times that late work is not accepted and they know that the teacher enforces that standard.

(6) The fifth grade science teacher collected papers from the students who had each written a summary of the science fair project they would like to do. The paper was assigned two days ago. A lot of work was done in class about how to organize and how to explain a science fair project. Each student turned in the

assignment. As the teacher collected the papers individually, she could tell that very good work had been done.

(7) The experienced fourth grade teacher knew from her 24 years in the classroom that the traditional Friday spelling test was an important part of guiding students toward mastery of new vocabulary and toward mastery of spelling. In recent years, students struggled more with spelling than students used to. Could computers, cell phones, and text message usage explain the increased spelling difficulties? The teacher asked friends who taught middle school and high school classes if the older students finally learned to spell well. The clear answer was that spelling was not a strong skill as it had been for earlier generations.

(8) Students at one middle school move up to the next grade if they pass six of their seven classes in the current grade. When the assistant principal asked a student why he made B and C grades in six classes, but had a grade of F in one other class, the answer was, "Oh, that's the class I decided to fail. I don't need it. I can still pass for the year if I fail that class." Reality for that student and for some other students was to decide to fail a class, although the students were perfectly capable of succeeding in the chosen class.

(9) "Great work! Very impressive writing. You showed a thorough understanding of the facts and the ideas. You established an overall thesis and you proved the thesis with much accurate historical evidence. Read all of the comments. See me with any questions." The tenth grade World History teacher had invested five hours in grading a set of test papers from one class of 25 World History students. The results were very favorable.

(10) The seventh grade class discussion about the presidential election process was lively, with much participation and interest. The results would have been

better if these interruptions had not happened: a public address announcement telling one group of students to go to the bus loading area for transportation to their field trip destination; a phone call from the office asking for two students to meet now with an assistant principal; a knock on the door with a student office assistant bringing a letter from the office for a student; a public address announcement telling one student who must be skipping class to return to class; a phone call from a teacher who needed to get a message about an after school activity to a student; a public address statement telling all teachers to check their e-mail now. Each of these interruptions disrupted instruction, learning, the work of students, and the work of teachers.

(11) When asked by a visitor to a high school, "What is the biggest problem teachers have to deal with," one teacher replied, "Cell phones." When asked to explain that, the teacher said, "Some students, actually many students, seem to be addicted to cell phones. They use them between classes. They try to sneak some looks at them during class. They try to use them during class and some just dare you to do anything about it. Their minds are on the most recent text message, not the current topic in our class."

(12) Another teacher replied to the question about the biggest problem she faced daily by saying, "The students increasingly will not read. I give them a short two-page article to read and the next day they cannot answer questions about it. Do they have the ability to read? Of course they do. Are they willing to make the effort to read and think and analyze? Fewer and fewer students do that. Where did the work ethic go?"

(13) An experienced eight grade U.S. History teacher was asked what had changed most during his 28 years of teaching. "The internet. Students used to write a serious eight-page research paper in eighth grade. They

read books and articles and original historical documents. Now students think that research is copying whatever shows up on the website at the top of the list on the first page of an internet search."

Do taxpayers know the reality of what occurs in the schools they pay for? Do parents and guardians know the reality of what occurs in the schools they pay taxes for? Do those groups spend time in the schools they pay taxes for? Do they spend enough time at school to get a thorough awareness of what takes place at school? Do they regularly communicate with people who work at school? If the answer is yes to those questions, the opportunity for a school to reach bestness is greatly enhanced.

Do lawmakers, policy makers, and regulation writers know the reality of what occurs daily at the schools they make laws, policies, or regulations for?

In order to know what reality is at a school, nothing can be assumed. Conditions at schools now are not what they were two generations ago, one generation ago, 10 years ago or five years ago. Should decisions impacting a school be based on reality or unreality? The answer, of course, is reality. Knowing reality requires being at school often and frequently listening to people who work daily at school. This proximity combined with listening enables decision makers to base their conclusions on reality instead of unreality.

School reality and classroom reality cannot be clearly seen, known, understood, or related to from a distance. There are no students in the education bureaucracy's office buildings. There are no classrooms in the education hierarchy's bureaus, divisions or departments. Reality is not hiding. School reality and classroom reality are displayed vividly in school and in classrooms for anyone who makes the effort to see, to realize, and to comprehend.

Is school reality found in numbers, statistics, and

data? No. Numbers, statistics, and data can be useful tools for reality seekers, but the benefits of charts, graphs, and other numerical measurements are limited. Attendance at an elementary school one year averaged 97 percent and the next year averaged 96 percent. What does the 1 percent decline mean? Who was absent? Was everyone absent occasionally or were some students absent many times while other students were absent rarely or never? What caused the absences? Were any families of frequently absent students contacted so reasons for absences could be resolved and so attendance could be improved? Look beyond the overall numbers. Look at people.

A test is given to evaluate reading skills of fourth graders. The results are available for each student, but are evaluated mostly by demographic groups. The highest individual score is from a student who is in the lowest scoring group. The lowest individual score is from a student who is in the highest scoring group. The school's highest achieving reader does not need the remedial reading program that is recommended for the lowest scoring group. The school's lowest achieving reader cannot function in the advanced reading program that is recommended for the highest reading group. Reality is not found in the broad-based group statistics. Reality of student achievement is found one student at a time. Students, teachers, schools, and school reality are much more than any quantitative evaluation can measure in full.

When current students or former students are asked, "Who or what at school made the most important impact on your education?", the answer is not about a law, a regulation, or a policy. The answer is about a person, perhaps a teacher, a school counselor, a principal or an assistant principal. Laws, regulations, and policies are needed, but their helpful impact on individual students is often limited or is less than was intended. The reality at school is that the most powerful variable, resource, action, method, or program is of, by and for people. Honorable, ethical, professional, productive, direct human action is the ultimate resource of the best school.

Many teaching trends are temporary, counter-productive, experimental, destructive wastes of time and wastes of money. The best school uses proven teaching methods that work. The best school does not fall for what gets promoted most by the education reform industry and the professional development industry.

Reality confirms, unfortunately, that some very serious misbehavior, some crimes, and some dangerous situations can occur at school. The best school is serious about school security. School law enforcement officers or school resource officers, or other school authorities with similar duties, are very visible at the best school as reassurance to and protection for the well-behaved students and as support for and protection for the adults. Those officers or other school authorities are there also to prevent wrongdoing when possible or to resolve it when necessary.

Any school that endeavors to reach the level of the best school must constantly confront reality. Problems cannot be overlooked with an attitude of "It could be worse" or "That's just the way things are". Problems are identified, analyzed, understood, confronted, and solved at the best school.

Proper successes and achievements must not be overlooked, but are celebrated and are analyzed. The celebrations help confirm what the school's priorities are. Analysis reveals what caused the successes and achievements so those insights can be applied to school situations which are not yet successes, which are not yet the best.

Confronting reality does not require pessimism or cynicism; rather, it is intended to be practical, pragmatic, and direct. Progress begins with a thorough and accurate understanding of reality.

Education is energized in part by a bold hope that all

students can and will accomplish significant learning. For that hope to be manifested in actual deeds and results, reality must be confronted continuously. At the best school, today's reality is fully known, but is not fully accepted as the ultimate level of possible achievement.

Magnificent dreams can inspire people. Realistic actions that cause the dreams to come true can abundantly and beneficially impact people. Lofty ideals float away unless they are implemented with down-to-earth, realistic, practical, feasible, effective, honorable actions. The best school takes many small steps each day toward very large goals.

The world of education has many fascinating philosophies and many intriguing theories. Some of these concepts are worth reading about, discussing, and contemplating; however, philosophies and theories will not solve problems at school. The best school is not in a perpetual race from one philosophy of learning to a new theory of management to a different philosophy of teaching to a newer theory of leadership. The best school is guided by a clear purpose and concentrates its efforts on actions that fulfill the purpose.

The best school is a place of purposeful action based on realistic appraisal of what works best to accomplish what matters most.

It is utterly futile, nonsensical, unethical, unproductive, harmful, unprofessional, and wrong to impose misguided, unrealistic, unnecessary mandates, directives, and reforms on schools. The actions that are often forced upon schools to "fix the problems of education" can fail to solve those problems and can cause new problems.

Cynics might think that the education reform machine intentionally evades reality, creates certain-to-fail schemes, and then creates a new certain-to-fail scheme just to perpetuate the continuance of the education reform business. To the extent that any of the cynical perceptions are accurate, the education reform business owes an apology to people who work at schools and who must endure the repeated mistakes of education reform efforts, schemes, gimmicks, and distortions.

Many people express a concern about the quality of schools. Many interest groups, community organizations, political parties, politicians, parents, guardians, business leaders, and others express general concern about various aspects of current educational results. These people would like to help schools improve and that honorable goal has merit.

For that goal to be reached, though, the people who seek to improve schools must know the current reality at school. That reality provides the only valid starting point for serious consideration of actions that could be implemented to improve the school.

We know what works. We can identify reality at any school. Then people can reason together to decide what actions are needed and what actions are not needed. A shared understanding of school reality is the smart place to start in the process of becoming the best school and in continuing to be the best school.

When everyone who is concerned about a school, is involved in any way with a school, or is working at a school can share an accurate understanding of school reality, the work which follows can be more harmonious, productive, and purposeful. In truth, it can be the best work and it can help produce the best school.

TEACHING: THE ESSENTIAL WORK
AT THE BEST SCHOOL

There are many factors and many variables which impact children and teenagers that are beyond the control of educators. One of those components is time. Consider an academic year consisting of 180 school days with students at school for seven hours daily. 180 times seven equals 1,260. 365 times 24 equals 8,760. The conclusion is that students are at school for 1,260 hours out of the 8,760 hours in a calendar year. That equals 14.4 percent of the year.

Include an average of one hour per school day of homework and one hour per school day of travel to and from school including early arrival at school prior to the start of the school day and 360 hours are added to the 1,260 hours. 1,620 total school-related hours divided by the 8,760 hours in a calendar year reveals the school gets 18.5 percent of a student's time.

No doubt, some students invest much more than one hour per school day on homework, but other students spend little or no time on homework. These calculations do omit extracurricular activities such as sports or clubs.

Whether the number is 14.4 percent or 18.5 percent, the outcome is obvious: time at school and additional time connected with school amount to a small, limited portion of the time in each year for children and for teenagers. Because of this time reality, the best school makes each minute at school count for what matters most. There is no time to waste.

This is not to suggest that an obsessive workaholic pace is needed at the best school. This is to affirm that at the best school every minute matters. This is to affirm that at the best school every minute of instructional time is invested in productive activity that causes learning. Of course, time is required for lunch or for moving from one classroom to another during class change time, yet time scheduled for academic instruction is applied productively and is protected from any attempt to misdirect or to steal that time.

Of all the factors and variables which impact children and teenagers that educators can control, the most important one is what happens in classrooms so teaching which causes learning occurs. Educators cannot control what families allow their children and teenagers to do away from school. Educators cannot control what children and teenagers do away from school that their families do not allow, but that happens nonetheless. Educators cannot control how many hours older students work at part-time jobs. Educators cannot control the examples set by, the priorities established by, the rules enforced by, or the circumstances of families which send children and teenagers to school.

Educators can control the educational activities, the instructional methods, and the teaching actions which occur in classrooms. Will some students work at school harder, more seriously, with better attention, and with better behavior than other students? Yes. At the best school, excuses are not tolerated and persistent, determined, relentless efforts continue with the goal that every student will learn. Yet, the best school is a school, a place for academic work. The best school is not designed to, staffed to, or organized to resolve every issue which can impact children and teenagers.

One goal of educators in recent years has been that each high school graduate will be "college or career-ready." Schools have important and vital work to do so that goal is reached. Families of students have equal or greater work to do so that goal is reached. When families make sure that their children and teenagers are school-ready each day, the results at school improve. If a family fails in that responsibility, it is unrealistic and impractical to require or to expect that a school can compensate fully for what a family does not accomplish day-to-day. Schools are schools. Families are families. When families and schools team up on education, the work is symbiotic and the results are multiplied.

We know what works in the classroom. Think of the best teacher you ever had. Perhaps that best teacher taught you in elementary school, in middle school, in high school, in college, or in graduate school. What did your best teacher do that was so impactful, so effective, and so memorable?

The point is that we know what the best teachers do, so at the best school all teachers do what the best teachers have always done to get results in proper, professional, honorable, ethical ways. At the best school, each teacher is expected to reach the level of bestness. At the best school, each teacher expects of himself or herself to reach and to maintain the level of bestness.

Is each teacher at the best school a clone of, a duplicate of, a copy of, an imitation of one exact model of teaching? No. Is any teacher at the best school an independent, nonconforming, creatively wayward academic traveler who erratically wanders through a disconnected series of instructional methods or non-instructional activities? No.

17

The best school has a clearly identified curriculum which specifies what students at certain grade levels and in particular subjects need to learn. The best school also has an approved, but not finite, list of classroom teaching methods and activities. This list is not finite because some useful innovations or teachable moment opportunities can arise; however, one standard never changes: do what works best to accomplish what matters most, which is to cause learning.

At the best school, teachers often trade successes and good ideas. A faculty meeting at the best school could spend most of the meeting time with several teachers presenting their most effective teaching activities. The teachers at the best school do not work in total isolation; rather, time is purposefully allocated so teachers can observe each other teaching, can exchange lesson plans, can hear about successes, can answer questions about why a certain instructional activity did not work as it was expected to, and can productively interact as part of doing their job.

Teachers at the best school are observed regularly by the school's principal and assistant principal(s). These school leaders know what is taking place in the classrooms at their school. These school leaders never settle for the minimum requirement which may simply necessitate two, three, or four observations of a teacher during one school year. The leaders of the best school visit some classrooms as an on-going part of their daily duties. These visits are not two-minute condensed, superficial, pointless, check-list managed walk-throughs; rather, they are significant, substantial, thorough, and meaningful with interaction and with follow-up communication in person.

The best school frequently measures learning results. Valid and reliable tests from outside sources are used occasionally, but the day-to-day grading of student work is given more emphasis than an annual or periodic snapshot test score.

The best school has a demanding grading scale. The best school finds it is unacceptable to endorse a grade of 60 percent, 65 percent, or 70 percent as passing. To accept those levels would mean that a student passes a class without knowing 40 percent, 35 percent, or 30 percent of the required academic content. The best school prefers not to have a grading scale which includes the letter grade of "D". The best school asks boldly, "Where else in society would a grade of D be tolerated? Do people accept a D-level of service when a car is repaired, when a prescription is filled, or when a restaurant meal is presented?"

As a school works toward reaching the level of the best school, it can decide to abandon the old grading scale that tolerated 60 percent or 65 percent or 70 percent as passing. Raising the minimum passing grade to 75 percent or 80 percent does not cause fear that a higher number of students will fail. Instead, this action inspires dedication to being the best and this action energizes a commitment to find the steps which will lead previously low performing students to the new, higher requirements. This action also sends a clear message to students that doing school work is a serious responsibility of students.

The best school helps students understand that meeting or surpassing the standards of the more demanding grading scale is in their best interest. The students will be known by future employers, by colleges, or by technical schools as already having succeeded at a more challenging school.

At the best school, grades are earned and the performance standards to earn those grades are high. Great grades are not given merely for showing up, for completing an assignment, or for making an effort. Great grades are earned for results that meet or exceed challenging standards. Earning grades means that there is no extra credit.

At the best school, teachers pay attention to details such as this: spelling counts. "But you know what word I meant," is not persuasive. At the best school, details such as spelling, turning work in on time, and doing all assignments completely are non-negotiable.

The best school does not impose useless, pointless, superficial, senseless professional development programs on teachers. Money and time are not wasted on absolutely nonsensical, trendy, dense schemes, programs, initiatives, or tasks. At the best school, every effort is made so the time of and the work of teachers is devoted to teaching, which causes learning. Uses of time and of work effort which do not cause learning are not imposed on teachers at the best school.

In exchange for protecting teachers from any classroom invasions or sabotage that would waste classroom time, the best school requires teachers to get results. Of course, the best teachers already require themselves to get results and they already will settle for nothing less than the best.

Teachers at the best school do not abandon academic traditions which have worked for a long time simply because those traditions are associated with an earlier era. Teachers at the best school provide for their students the superior combination of what has worked always plus very selective, proven, effective, useful innovations. At the best school, innovations are not used merely because they are new, are packaged well, are marketed persuasively, are politically correct, or have a current popular image. Innovations are used when they are proven to get better results than established methods get.

Teachers at the best school know that doing mathematics from addition to algebra with pencil and paper forces a certain type of thinking which shows what the numbers are doing and which strengthens understanding of what the numbers mean. Simply pushing buttons on a gadget while creating an answer can provide an answer, but does not nurture an understanding of what the answer means or whether the answer makes sense.

"But why do I have to memorize the Preamble to the Constitution? I can look it up on my phone. Why isn't that good enough?" When asked that question by a student at the best school, a teacher can reply confidently: "You are more than your phone. The goal is not just to look it up and see the words on a screen. The goal is to see the words in your mind and to fully interact in your brain with the meaning of those words. Once you memorize those words, they become a part of you and of your increasing knowledge. We do more than just know how to access the words. We know how to analyze the words, interact with the words, make sense of the words, and take ideas from the words. The first step in this particular learning activity is to commit the words to memory. You can do that."

Teachers at the best school have difficult, demanding, tiring, important work to do. These teachers are not satisfied with personally reaching the level of a best teacher, while working in an ordinary or in a failing school. Teachers at the best school expect a work environment which accepts nothing less than the best from each person individually, from all people collectively, in each classroom, in all classrooms, throughout every part of the school, and with every decision or action at the school.

Being the best school is the result of the school's totality with each person consistently contributing his or her bestness in a workplace where the best is desired by everyone, supported for everyone, and celebrated by everyone. Is that asking a lot? Yes. It is asking for the best. Anything less is unacceptable. Why experience school or anything else with a standard that is less that the best?

That sounds challenging and difficult. Yes, it is. That also sounds worthwhile, meaningful, and inspiring. Yes, it is.

Teachers at the best school abide by some "do" and some "do not" guidelines. Among the do items are the following: do cause learning daily; with reasonable exceptions for large projects and long papers, do return student work within one to three days of when it was turned in and include useful comments on those papers to individualize instruction; do build upon the strengths of your students; do address the weaknesses of your students; do challenge your students; do require proper behavior of your students; do create instructional materials for your students; do what works knowing that what works with one group of students may not work with another group; do continue your personal learning about the subjects you teach and about how to best teach those subjects; do take very good care of yourself; do enforce rules; do document classroom situations that concern you; and do keep school leaders aware of classroom problems.

Among the do not items are the following: do not rely on pre-packaged, generic, ordinary instructional materials that come with textbooks; do not use video after video, day after day; do not distribute work for students to do while you do something at your desk and ignore the students; do not make rules which students are allowed to violate without a penalty; do not accept excuses from students; do not arrive late to school and leave early from school; do not give coaching or other supplemental duties more effort, attention, work, and priority than you give to teaching; do not leave students in your classroom unattended; do not give extra credit work because it makes students think they can make up for past irresponsibility by desperately doing some other tasks; do not use vulgar language; do not let anger over student misbehavior lead you to unprofessional words or actions; do not assume that parents or guardians are told much about school by students, especially as students enter middle school or high school; do not teach unless you can make a complete commitment to being the best teacher.

The best school makes a formal, professional, and serious pledge to provide all workplace conditions in which any willing teacher can reach the level of the best teacher. Reciprocally, teachers at the best school make a formal, professional, and serious pledge to cause learning to occur within each of their students. This symbiotic bond is essential for attaining and remaining at the level of the best school.

P.S. Some educators favor the use of extra credit work. The author of this book opposes it. These different perspectives – on this topic and others – create a splendid opportunity to think, to identify the best. What is the goal of extra credit? Does extra credit reach that goal? Are there better ways to reach that goal? To be the best, it is important to think, think more, and keep thinking.

3

STUDENTS: DO WHAT IS RIGHT.
WORK. THINK. LEARN. BE POLITE.

Students, you must do the school work which is assigned to you. You must obey the school rules and the classroom rules which are explained to you. You must discipline yourselves so that at all times during your education you do what is right, you work, you think, you learn, and you are polite. These duties are your responsibility. Do not make excuses. Do get results. You are not being given options or choices. You are being given duties and responsibilities. At the best school, we are very serious about your education. At the best school, you must be very serious about your education.

Your responsibilities will increase in complexity as your age increases; however, from the moment you begin kindergarten through the moment you graduate from high school, it is your responsibility to do what is right, to work, to think, to learn, and to be polite. Is that requiring a lot? Yes. Are you capable of doing all of that? Yes. Anything less is unacceptable to us and is unfair to you.

Do what is right, work, think, learn and be polite are

disciplines which will serve you now and throughout your life. They are required for your success at school. They apply to other parts of your life now as they will apply to your life after high school graduation. Master those skills now and use them forever.

Educational opportunities will be presented to you persistently and effectively, but education will not be acquired by you effortlessly. You will not absorb wisdom, knowledge, facts, information, and other benefits of education simply by sitting in a classroom for 13 years during elementary school, middle school, and high school. You have work which you must do daily for 13 years of school.

Immediately upon learning how to read, this is a permanent, never-ending assignment for you: read, read more, keep reading. Reading is the path to anywhere and to everywhere.

The reading assignments you are given will increase in length and in complexity as you progress through your years in school. Read all assigned material at least once, but when you read material twice you will learn more, you will learn better, and you will give yourself an advantage.

Especially as you advance through elementary school to middle school and then to high school, if your school is the best school you should expect few second chances or other alternatives to doing what you were supposed to do the first time. Learning to be responsible means realizing that there are proper ways to do work and a proper schedule for completing work. You are not expected or required to be perfect. You are expected and required to be the best. By the final year of middle school, you will have realized that second chances have, for the most part, faded away.

Being the best student at the best school includes doing your work completely and on time. Mistakes in the work can lead to new instruction and to new learning. Irresponsibility, as seen in not working, is unacceptable because it accomplishes nothing. Make no excuses. They weaken you and they are to be rejected. Get results. They strengthen you and they are admired. Perfection is not the goal. Complete commitment to doing the work which leads to being the best is the goal. When you do the best work you can do and still do not understand something, your teacher will show you another way to understand it.

Student responsibility is rarely mentioned when critics of schools indict education for its shortcomings. Those critics miss an important factor, perhaps because they are not in schools dealing with daily school reality where this factor is obvious: some students steal.

Some student thieves steal possessions from other students, from adults, or from the school. Serious disciplinary action is needed.

Some students steal time. They intentionally and repeatedly disrupt in classrooms, thus limiting instruction for everyone else. This steals time from the teacher who must now spend it dealing with the disruptive student. This is time that should be invested in teaching all students in the classroom. This misbehavior is stealing instructional time from the other students. This misbehaving student is stealing from taxpayers who expect their money to be invested in education, not stolen by a child or a teenager who disrupts a classroom.

At the best school, theft is not tolerated. Certain and effective action is taken to penalize any student who steals. At the best school, theft is rare because everyone knows that stealing is beneath them and that any thief will learn quickly and clearly not to repeat that violation.

The best school is quite capitalistic in recognition of students who attain impressive academic achievement and in recognition of proper student behavior. The best school implements the capitalistic concept of "we get more of what we reward." For students who consistently do what is right, work, think, learn, and are polite, there are earned rewards and recognitions.

Retail stores reward frequent shoppers. Airlines reward frequent fliers. Hotels and motels reward frequent visitors. The best school rewards or recognizes students whose academic achievement is superior; whose academic achievement shows significant and sustained improvement; whose work ethic is outstanding; and whose proper manners and behavior are exemplary.

At the best school, students know that when they do what is wrong they will be punished. Students also know that when they consistently do what is right they do not merely avoid punishment; rather, they are recognized and rewarded. This is capitalistic. This is effective. This celebrates hard work, strong results, and exemplary behavior. This is part of the atmosphere, the personality, and the way of life at the best school.

Students at the best school know not to ask for extra credit. Part of the capitalist approach at the best school is that grades are earned, never given. Students know they must keep up day-to-day. There will never be any magical extra credit to replace work that should have been done earlier as it was assigned originally.

Students at the best school know that additional learning opportunities are provided if a student worked hard, but just did not understand the topic that was studied. The teacher and the student will work anew to master the topic. Students know that the student must always make a complete effort. Modified learning opportunities come when despite complete effort, the desired learning has not yet occurred. Students know that their work ethic must always be the best. Because the best school seeks the best results for students, it accepts nothing less than the best effort from students.

The best school promotes student responsibility and does not take actions that could encourage student irresponsibility. In the category of gaps at school, the best school closes the responsibility gap and in doing that closes the results gap. This is done individually so any gap between a student's current performance and the student's potential performance is noticed, is measured, and is closed.

Students at the best school are aware that assignments are due at the start of class on the due date. Leaving school before class or arriving late after class on the due date does not change the due date. Work must be turned in upon arrival at school if the class was missed or before leaving school if the class will be missed.

The best school promotes a Triple 10 concept. Consider a scale of zero to 10 for work ethic, for manners, and for results. The goal is to reach the level of 10 in each of these three categories which means 10, 10, 10 or what the best school calls Triple 10. This is the standard for everyone at the best school.

The parents or guardians of students at the best school are told to visit school during the school day so they can attend class occasionally. The best school initiates much communication with families using all available communication methods. The best school monitors parent or guardian visits to school and inquires when a family has not been to school, or at least been in touch with someone at school, for a month.

Students at the best school are taught precise communication skills for written work and for verbal presentations. Social media and text message abbreviations or jargon are prohibited in school work. Spelling counts. Verbal imprecision such as endless use of the words "like," "stuff," or "thing" is avoided. Verbal communication includes please, thank you, and not interrupting other people. Vulgar language is 100 percent prohibited. Students are told that popular culture's obsession with vulgarity and with other improper conduct are seen as the opposites of the desired actions at the best school.

Students at the best school experience a wholesome, designed, beneficial process called studentization. The studentization process at the best school is a combination of teaching and training. The goal is for each student to master the skills of a successful student.

Has every student at every school mastered the skills which are needed for success as a student? No. Are the skills associated with successful students held as secrets by some young scholars? No. At the best school, these skills are taught to everyone using an exact process of studentization.

Does education include a specific process of studentization which is training students in the skills, methods, habits, and actions of successful students? It does at the best school. Academic subjects are taught as well as they should be and must be. Literacy is taught as it must be. Yet, no matter what subjects are taught, to fully learn the academic content of a subject, a student must know how to be an accomplished, productive, disciplined, organized student. With a solid foundation in student skills mastered through a studentization process, overall learning is increased.

When people are trained, the goal is for everyone to obtain the same information and the same skills. When a team of firefighters arrives at the scene of an emergency, they follow their training. It is not a time for each firefighter to create individual firefighting actions. Each person individually and the group collectively must do what they were trained to do. When the crisis is resolved, there will be time to evaluate and perhaps to suggest improvements, but until then, follow the training.

The skills, the actions, the habits, and the standards of very successful students are clearly known. At the best school, the benefits of these skills are taught and the students are trained to master these skills.

Some of the skills which are taught in the studentization process are age-specific for students in elementary school, in middle school, or in high school. Other studentization skills are applicable across age groups.

Time management. Punctuality. Completing work on time. Following school rules and classroom instructions. Organizing school materials. Enhancing reading and reading comprehension. Paying total attention in class. Properly participating in class discussions. Taking notes. Studying effectively. Research procedures including source selection and citing sources. Setting priorities. Managing and completing homework. Doing your own work, not copying. Being honest about the work you do, not cheating. These are some of the skills which the best school makes sure that all students acquire through a direct instructional process and a precisely designed process of studentization.

The fundamentals of studentization are required to be applied in each classroom. Some teachers may add further skills which are necessary for their grade level and/or for their subject matter; however, students at the best school know that the foundational skills of studentization are to be used in each classroom.

At the best school being a student is seen as a combination of duty, responsibility, job, opportunity, and adventure. Each adult at the best school has a clearly described job. Each student at the best school also has a clear job description and is individually evaluated in terms of that job description. This is part of what makes the best school the best school. This is part of what causes students at the best school to do what is right, work, think, learn, and be polite.

4

LEADERSHIP AND MANAGEMENT: SET THE EXAMPLE

Educators who have leadership and/or management authority at the best school abide by these standards: do what you require your colleagues to do; be what you require your colleagues to be; avoid what you require your colleagues to avoid.

The idea emerges that the best school is deliberately and purposefully structured. That is accurate. Structure is the foundation of productivity, of achievement, and of results. Is there room for creativity and innovation at the best school? Yes, yet those are done within and upon a structure. Plus, those are done to enhance the purpose of the best school which is, of course, to cause learning.

Bestness permeates the best school. All that is done at the best school is done at the level of, the quality of, the standard of, and the performance of the best. This occurs only through a conscious and continuous effort which is planned, designed, implemented, managed, led, evaluated, and, when needed, improved.

People in positions of leadership and/or management

duties at the best school exemplify, personify, support, inspire, and acknowledge the characteristics, the traits, the minute-to-minute way of working, the communication methods, the work ethic, the people skills, the behavior, and the manners which are compulsory and indispensable for everyone at the best school.

At some schools, the educators who work there are divided into categories such as teachers, counselors, librarians, school administrators and other positions. Another categorization system could be between the educators who work in classrooms full-time and the educators who do not work in classrooms full-time.

At the best school, all of the educators work in classrooms and for classrooms. The difference is that some educators work in a classroom during the entire day while other educators work in classrooms during part of the day while working for classrooms the rest of the day.

Principals, assistant principals, and counselors have many leadership duties and management responsibilities which are done in school offices, during meetings, in parts of the building or campus which need supervision, on the telephone, or with use of a computer. These responsibilities are essential to a properly functioning school; however, these tasks must not prevent principals, assistant principals, or counselors from being in classrooms regularly.

At the best school, principals, assistant principals, school counselors, academic deans, instructional coaches, or educators with any title expect themselves to be in classrooms daily. This daily classroom presence and involvement is not seen as interfering with other leadership and management responsibilities they have; rather, this classroom work is seen as the top priority which all other tasks support.

The leaders and managers of the best school continually develop talent and skills of faculty and staff. The best school never allows ability to go unused if already present or to be undeveloped if not already present.

The best school creates career opportunities rather than giving only two major options of teach or be a school administrator. Teachers can be given management and leadership duties which go beyond their one classroom. Teachers who are aspiring school administrators can be mentored by the principal and the assistant principal(s). Conversely, school administrators and school counselors could teach a class in addition to being in multiple classrooms daily. This approach may seem to be atypical, but it is a strength of the best school.

There are some circumstances which unexpectedly occur at a school. The school leaders must immediately stop what they are doing and intervene to resolve these difficulties. The best school is not immune to or isolated from such problematic events; however, at the best school these events are outliers. The educators at the best school work harmoniously to stop a problem at its earliest stage, although the higher goal is to prevent problems whenever possible.

One action which helps the leaders and the managers of the best school prevent problems is by being everywhere throughout the school at all times. If that seems to be physically impossible, think again please. When each principal, assistant principal, school counselor, and other educators at school who are not in classrooms full-time invest time each hour of the school day, perhaps on a shared and rotational basis, in being throughout the school building, one ideal result can be the prevention of problems or the result is the intervention in a problem at its early stage. At the best school, education leaders and managers prefer to pre-act than to react.

The leaders and managers of the best school know what faculty members and staff members are doing each day by supportively interacting with them. For these exemplary educators, a minimum required two, three or four classroom observations per year to evaluate a teacher would be unacceptable and embarrassing. The leaders and managers of the best school spend a lot of each day out and about interacting with people in all parts of the school. How else could they properly lead and manage?

In this chapter, the terms leaders and managers are used more than the common term, school administrators. Why? Because leadership and management done well are more comprehensive and are more effective than what is usually associated with the term school administration. Leadership and management are skills used in large corporations, in small businesses, in hospitals, in non-profit organizations, and in other parts of society. School leaders and managers at the best school master the body of knowledge within school administration and apply the broader body of knowledge within the totality of leadership and management. A school is not a factory or a corporation, so adjustments in how leadership and management are implemented at school must be made; however, leadership and management wisdom from sources other than school administration should not be overlooked.

Leaders and managers of the best school know that education does not have the problem of too little data. These educators know that schools can get lost in the maze of data and that schools can mistakenly think that education is about numbers. Education is about people learning. Numbers can help, but there should not be a dictatorship of excessive data. It is better to have fewer numbers combined with more useful analysis of what the important numbers mean or reveal. Endless numbers that lead to nothing useful or applicable is a situation to be avoided at the best school.

The leaders and managers of the best school make sure that school itself is a wholesome workplace. The building is safe; the building is maintained so all systems function correctly; the building is clean; people never run out of needed supplies; preventive maintenance is done on the heating/ventilation/air conditioning system; the copy machines work; the technology devices and infrastructure function; back-up power sources are available.

A wholesome workplace also means that actions which would interrupt instruction are prevented. Vulgar language by anyone at school is not tolerated. Students are required to talk to and act toward adults respectfully and politely. Adults act and speak professionally.

The leaders and managers at the best school eagerly, sincerely, and frequently acknowledge superior work done by students, teachers, staff and other people at school. Some acknowledgment may be as simple as spoken words of appreciation while other actions may be more elaborate. The best school celebrates its bestness and creates momentum for continued bestness.

The best school's leaders and managers promote from within whenever that is the right decision. When talent at the school is continually being developed, promoting from within can be the norm. If capable people who seek new challenges and expanded career opportunities are denied those experiences, a school causes unnecessary discouragement and frustration. This can end with highly capable educators going elsewhere to work. That does not happen to the educators at the best school due to enlightened personnel decision making by the school's leadership and management.

At the best school, leaders and managers seek student ideas, input, and perspective; however, this input is filtered through the fact that students are not trained in evaluating teaching in particular or schools in general. Student input is welcomed and is obtained, but it is not the sole basis for action.

Leaders and managers at the best school communicate in person whenever possible and via e-mail when that option is adequate. The best school is a personal place much more than it is an electronic place. At the best school, the people control the technology. The technology never controls the people. Of course, technology is used and for some communication and tasks, technology options are sufficient. Still, direct, personal, and interpersonal communication is preferred at the best school.

The emerging best school's leaders and managers have no tolerance of unprofessional action by any adult at school. The principal and the assistant principal(s) of the emerging best school are aware of and take proper action about teachers who leave their classroom unattended while students are there; who show too many videos; who work a minimal amount; who spend teaching time on coaching or other supplemental duties while students do endless and pointless worksheets that a student aide "grades."

It is a mistake, it is negligence, it is misleadership, and it is mismanagement for principals and for assistant principals to assume that the actions of every person at a school, including at the best school, will automatically always align with complete commitment to and with full implementation of the school purpose. People should work correctly and many people do, but life does not always happen as it should due to the human variable. Effective leadership and effective management can help create and maintain bestness through very specific, purposeful, and intentional actions or interventions.

Ideally, the motivation to do the best work comes from the conscience of each person, but leaders and managers must be prepared to bring any currently wayward person back to what that person should have done. If work performance continues to be unacceptable, policies and procedures to address that problem must be followed fully.

The leaders and managers of the best school know that leadership and management work is not done only by principals and assistant principals. This is not to invite a coup. This is to strengthen the total team of professional educators and support staff who work at the best school. Teachers lead and manage instruction in their classrooms.

School counselors and other educators at school lead and manage within their duties. The same high standard is needed from and by other staff members.

All leadership and management efforts must consistently work to support and to implement the school purpose. The best school is not 25, 50, 100, 150 or more adults functioning as autonomous autocrats each moving in a different direction. Instead, those educators and staff members work in harmony as authorized, developed, guided, supported, encouraged leaders and managers who individually and collectively get results which add up to the best.

The principal and the assistant principal(s) working as the overall leaders and managers of the best school can learn from other schools, but they do not copy, imitate, or mimic what works at other schools. This is not to reject good ideas, but this is to realize that no two schools are exactly alike; therefore, what works at one school, what is needed at one school, may not work and may not be needed at another school.

Working closely with people at the best school, leaders and managers build upon strengths, embrace opportunities, and solve problems. The best school's leaders and managers know that there are more available programs, innovations, technologies, initiatives and changes than are needed. The best school filters all of these using its school purpose as the decision making tool. The best school does what most effectively causes learning. For school leaders and school managers, this filter is their compass, their map, their set of directions, their organizational conscience.

School leaders and managers at the best school communicate without using education jargon, education acronyms, or bureaucratic scripted non-replies. Communication is clear, direct, understandable, human, humane, and proper. Leaders and managers communicate with students, colleagues, parents, guardians, and community members with precision, clarity, certainty, knowledge, confidence, good judgment and good manners.

Leaders and managers of the best school eliminate incentives for failure. Example – the high school student who intentionally does no work in a class during August through May, yet who seeks to attend summer school for a few weeks in June or July and with minimal effort hopes to get a passing grade. The best school tells students that summer school is for classes that students have not taken already. This means that summer school is for students to get ahead, to accelerate their pace, to enrich their education. Summer school is not a time to do what should have been done in the first place. This is made very clear to students early in the school year.

Another example – the middle school student who is promoted to the next grade by passing six of the seven required classes for the year. This promotion policy invites some students to intentionally fail a class. The best school requires that seven out of seven classes are passed and intervenes early in the school year to reverse the work of any student who is not at the passing level in any class.

In truth, the best school never accepts merely passing a class as adequate. Some schools might evaluate passing as good enough. For the best school, good enough is never tolerated. For the best school, only the best will suffice. The best school thinks of, seeks, implements, rewards, and celebrates the best standards, the best achievements, and the best results.

The leaders and managers of the best school are satisfied only with the best results of, by, and for everyone. Making that happen is challenging and difficult. Accepting less than the best is, to these leaders and managers, unethical and is an improper compromise. Pursuit of the best is honorable. Attaining the best is absolutely exhilarating. The only way to attain the best is to magnificently pursue the best with a complete commitment to reaching and maintaining bestness.

DAY-TO-DAY: MINUTES MATTER

At the best school, each minute is valued, prized, protected and productively invested. The educational experience of a student who completes kindergarten through high school graduation will involve 13 years at schools. Those 13 school years are the total of the minutes in each hour, during each day, throughout all years at school.

How many minutes is a student at school for academic instruction during those 13 years? Use these assumptions knowing that actual numbers vary by location: 180 school days, six hours of classroom instruction daily, and 13 years of education. 180 multiplied by six is 1,080 instructional hours in a school year which means 64,800 instructional minutes in a school year. Time for lunch and for time between classes is not included.

64,800 minutes per school year multiplied by 13 school years equals 842,400 minutes. With supportive school conditions and with effective teaching to cause learning, that means a student could encounter 842,400 minutes loaded with learning during 13 years of being a student. With each of those minutes filled effectively with learning causing experiences in classrooms, the amount of learning and the quality of learning are boundless. That idea maximizes the power of each minute at the best school.

The best school revolves around classrooms. The classroom is the center of the best school. It is in the classroom where the best school thrives. Classroom moments are protected from any interference and from interruptions unless a true event of urgency exists.

At the best school, classroom instructional time is not interfered with or interrupted by avoidable public address system usage, optional phone calls, unnecessary knocks on the door, or removing students from class for various non-instructional activities. All adults at the best school have a sign on their desk or at their work station which says, "Before taking any action ask yourself this question: What will be the impact on the work being done in classrooms? If the impact is negative, find another way."

The perspective of all adults at the best school is the viewpoint from the classroom. The classroom is the beating heart of the best school. The principal, the assistant principal(s), the librarian(s), the school counselor(s), and other educators who are not teachers, but who work at the best school, think in terms of what matters most in classrooms, what works best for the people in classrooms and what most supports the efforts in the classrooms.

Time is a precious resource which is not allowed to be wasted at the best school. Teachers at some schools may see faculty meetings as wastes of time. These wasted meetings occur because tradition dictates a regularly scheduled faculty meeting whether it is needed or not.

At the best school, faculty meetings are held to be of service to teachers. The faculty meeting agenda avoids anything that can be communicated as simple e-mail information and avoids anything that involves some interest group which for its motive seeks to be heard by teachers.

The intent of a faculty meeting should be either to

create opportunities for teachers to learn from each other as classroom successes are presented or to think collectively about school decisions that need in-depth faculty input. Faculty meetings are misused if they become announcement sessions. Common "for your information" announcements can be communicated sufficiently via e-mail so each person can read them on their schedule.

The best school is a professional learning workplace. All professional educators here learn together. Grade level or subject matter subsets of the overall school-wide professional learning workplace exist to enrich teachers and the classroom work they do, never merely to create a new organizational level for management purposes or directives.

The best school makes sure that professional development, also known as continuing education, is both professional and developmental. These programs are never superficial, trendy, pre-packaged, or generic. Professional development is presented using exemplary teaching methods. Professional development provides answers, insights, skills which educators have expressed a real need for, not which are imposed bureaucratically, autocratically, pointlessly or for political correctness.

During every minute of instructional time at the best school, students learn. Instruction begins at the moment class starts and instruction continues until the moment class ends. This is the standard for each class. School classes do not include free time. Weekends, evenings, and vacations have free time. The school day's instructional time is work time, learn time, and achieve time. The work and the work pace are not excessive, or overwhelming. The work and the work pace are vibrant, meaningful, and uplifting.

Are there any moments of enjoyment at the best school? Yes, but enjoyment is a by-product, not an objective. The intended product is learning. The experience of learning can be exhilarating, invigorating, and meaningful as learning brings satisfaction, joy, overcoming obstacles, surmounting challenges, and the pure delight of making progress. There are many smiles at the best school because there is much to smile about. Smiles are not the goal, yet when the true goal of learning is reached, there are abundant smiles.

Teacher time and professional integrity are respected. For example, teachers are not asked to fill out a psychological profile of a student. Teachers are not trained, certified, or licensed psychologists. Teachers are not asked to use time on a non-teaching task for which they do not have official credentials. At the best school, teachers teach.

At the best school, all of the adults arrive on time or early. The adults expect and require this schedule of themselves. This avoids the resentment and animosity at workplaces where some people constantly arrive late and/or leave early with no repercussions.

The minutes, each of the minutes, at the best school are productive. This is not a harmful, obsessive, rigid preoccupation with monitoring the minute hand on a clock. This is a wholesome, efficient, productive management of time. Taxpayers are not underwriting free time or any other wasted time. Time is a precious resource and when time is used wisely, results multiply. Age appropriate recess or similar activity scheduled outside of instructional time is an option which, if managed well, can enhance instructional time and can include some learning experiences.

"The comment you wrote on my test really meant a lot to me. Thanks for showing me how to be a better writer. And thanks for telling my parents how hard I'm working in your class." A student could make that statement only if a teacher invested a minute in writing the individualized comment on the student's essay test paper. Minutes matter. Minutes managed wisely and applied to causing learning get results. Thirteen years of well-managed minutes at school can produce 842,400 learning results for a student, one result and one minute at a time. Well-managed minutes are vital parts of bestness.

6

BUREAUCRACY: SUPPORT AND SERVICE

Education is of, by, and for people. Education, at its best, is an authentically human and humane endeavor. Education is not an assembly line process, a pre-fabricated set of scripted procedures, a formula, or a recipe.

Is education nebulous, indefinite, vague, or esoteric? No, education is designed, structured, and managed, yet with breathing room, with opportunities to explore, and with great vitality.

The overall education system has expanded to include a national government department of education, state departments of education, school districts or other local government management, plus multiple organizations or groups which seek to impact education. The task of the education bureaucracy and hierarchy is to do the important support work which helps the overall education system function with a constantly concentrated effort to cause learning rather than to create an organizational burden which becomes an abyss of procedural complexity.

The education bureaucracy has the vital roles of

support for and service to schools. When these roles are the prevailing priorities of the education bureaucracy, organizational hierarchy, or overall executive system, the benefits can be substantial. As with any bureaucracy or large organization, caution and vigilance are needed at all times to be sure that the bureaucracy does not become consumed with self-serving actions, circuitous meetings, vague task forces, or unproductive procedures. Policy making, regulation writing or re-writing, and re-organizations that create the appearance, the image, or the illusion of useful activity, but that get no real results, are avoided.

How can the bureaucracy most effectively provide service to and support for the best school? By seeing education itself and the supportive work done in the education bureaucracy from the classroom perspective. People who work in the education bureaucracy can ask themselves often, "How is what I am doing now providing service to and support for educators at schools so they maximize the learning of each student?" That question helps filter purposeful work from unneeded busy-ness.

The following guideline is an example of how a bureaucracy can maintain its singular concentration on what matters most: "It is the overall guiding standard of the Lombardy County Public Schools to listen to people who work at schools before we take action or make decisions. We will take only the actions which support each school's effort to become the best school." A similar guideline could be followed by state education officials, state political leaders, national education officials, and national political leaders to make sure that their efforts are supportive, helpful, practical, and productive.

Educators who work in the education bureaucracy, but who do not work at a school, can do much good for themselves and for schools by spending a lot of time in schools with emphasis on being in classrooms. How else can the fullness of school reality and classroom reality be known accurately? What better way is there to show service and support than by listening to, talking with, and working with the educators at school whom the education bureaucracy exists to serve and to support? What better way is there to reinforce the shared commitment to the commonly held purpose of causing learning?

Consider the example of the Chief Executive Officer (CEO) of a large restaurant chain. This executive regularly spends time in the restaurants. This executive actually spends some days each year working in the restaurants. This executive listens to, talks with, and interacts with employees and customers. This executive knows restaurant reality. There is no better use of this executive's time than to be in the restaurants often. No source of restaurant information can equal the reality check of being there. Of course, the CEO must be in the company offices often, but the CEO is not confined to the offices. The essence of the restaurant business is not in the company offices, it is in the restaurants. For education officials, the equivalent executive action is to be at schools often and to emphasize time in classrooms. The essence of education is at schools, especially in classrooms, not in centralized offices.

Education officials can, should and must set the example of selecting people for job openings based on merit. There is no tolerance of a good old boys and good old girls network in which friends hire friends and trade career favors. The best school district or education department service and support system selects the best people based objectively on merit.

The education hierarchy which most beneficially impacts schools has a serious skepticism of education trends and fads, of excessive mandated testing, and of sweeping reforms. These endeavors can often do much more harm than good. The enlightened education hierarchy does what serves and supports schools, not what is trendy, faddish, unnecessary, wasteful, or tumultuous.

The best education bureaucracy and hierarchy spend

some time carefully developing mission statements or vision statements. At the best organizations, these literary appeals never only get discussed, written, approved and then just set aside or referred to ceremonially. Instead, they provide guidance and they are followed.

More specifically and more oriented toward action is a clear, concise, precisely written one sentence statement of purpose which guides every decision and action. Example: the purpose of our school district (or education department) is to support efforts to cause learning by doing what matters most and what works best for students and for educators at schools.

The stereotypical image of the education bureaucracy and hierarchy by some, perhaps many, educators who work at a school is: "Those people never listen to us." "Those people could not do my job, but they insist on telling me how to do my job." "Why do they keep giving me more to do each year and why do they keep changing things every year?" "What do they do all day? Go to meetings and go to conferences while I work with students and plan lessons and grade papers and all the other stuff I have to do." "If they were serious, they would come substitute teach at least one day each month. Then they would know part of what we go through."

How is this divide bridged? How do the education bureaucracy and the education hierarchy work symbiotically with educators at schools? What actions could the education bureaucracy and the education hierarchy members take to better connect with the educators they are to serve and to support?

(1) Step one, spend much time in schools, especially in classrooms.
(2) Step two, listen to the educators who work in schools.
(3) Step three, communicate with educators at school to help them understand and realize how the support and service system functions.

(4) Step four, frequently repeat step one and step two.

There is every reason for the people who work at schools and the people who work in the education bureaucracy or hierarchy to team up, to work together, to share the same goals, and to know each other. That type of common commitment to a shared purpose is an essential part of the work that helps lead a school to become the best school and that helps lead many schools to bestness. It is also an essential way for the education bureaucracy and the education hierarchy to best provide service and support to schools.

For people who make laws, regulations, or policies about schools, following steps one and two shown above will produce a bountiful harvest of goodwill and good decisions. Give yourself the benefits of and share with other people the benefits of steps one and two. Remember, the process of solving a problem begins with an accurate and realistic identification of and understanding of the problem.

Elected political leaders who require of themselves that their work, which impacts education, includes much listening and includes taking only practical, purposeful action can further require that the education bureaucracy and education hierarchy also listen and also take only practical, purposeful action.

Political leaders who seek to improve education can help create the conditions which support and serve the best school. Examples of helpful action include the following: occasionally take one year and, unless there is an unavoidable urgency, pass no new laws, initiate no new programs, and implement no new mandates related to education. During this year, educators in schools can concentrate on teaching and will not have to apply any time or effort toward finding out how a new procedure works or merging that new procedure with every task they must do already.

During this moratorium year, political leaders can work with national, state, and local school officials – with input from educators at schools – to review existing laws, policies and regulations which deal with education. Some of these existing requirements are acceptable as is; some are harmful, counterproductive, or unnecessary and can be corrected or eliminated; some of the existing requirements may need to be replaced. Outdated laws, regulations, or policies can be eliminated. The goal will be to remove every part of each law, policy, and regulation which works against schools being able to concentrate on being the best school which does only what matters most and what works best to cause learning.

Of course, this year would include a renewed commitment to much listening to educators, especially to school level educators. This renewed commitment to listening would never end. When elected officials lead by listening, they set a vital example and greatly help enhance the best results for schools.

LAWS, REGULATIONS, AND POLICIES: QUALITY, NOT QUANTITY

When laws, regulations, and/or policies about education are considered, the wisdom and the standard of "first, do no harm" is a good filter. How can lawmakers, regulation writers, and policy makers avoid actions that are harmful despite intentions that are honorable? Screen any proposed law, regulation, or policy through the reality of current conditions in classrooms. How is that done? Prior to making any decision about new laws, new regulations, or new policies, get and utilize abundant insight from teachers and from other educators who work at schools.

The best school concentrates absolutely on what matters most and on what works best. Perpetual changes in laws, regulations, and policies about schools can force schools into being compliance machines when they should be academic learning centers.

Consider a conversation between a state legislator and a teacher:

Legislator: What is the best way for lawmakers to know

what schools need and what schools do not need? How can we be better informed?

Teacher: Great question. Here's an idea that would make political history and educational history. Take one school year and be a substitute teacher for one day each month. There could be a "Take the Legislators to School Day" where every member of the state Senate and the state House of Representatives would substitute teach. Maybe do that several times in a school year. Then the legislators could share their teaching experiences, their conversations with educators, and their overall observations with each other. The legislators would be better informed about education. The educators would be encouraged and could become better informed about how the state political process deals with education topics. The voters would be impressed. Everyone wins.

Legislator: That is perfectly sensible. It replaces some expensive and time-consuming education task force with real experience. We should go further so officials at the state's department of education and so people in school district central offices also substitute teach occasionally. We really need to do this. Half of the state budget is spent on schools. This would give us the opportunity to invest more time where that money is spent.

The best decisions about schools are made from a basis of complete, current, realistic understanding of conditions at each school now. Obtaining that understanding of a school requires being at school. There is no alternative to being there.

Can laws, regulations, and policies help schools reach the level of the best school? Yes. Can laws, regulations, and policies unintentionally complicate a school's effort to reach the best school status? Yes. One difference is the basis of the laws, the regulations, and the policies. If the basis is the current classroom reality, progress can be made and the pursuit of bestness can be enhanced. Actions that begin with reality and which helpfully address that reality are essential to supporting schools in becoming the best school.

A word about top-down, bureaucratic, trendy, faddish, mandated, costly, politically correct school reform: no. These massive upheavals do not work. For a school to be the best school, what does not work must be avoided and what does work must singularly be emphasized.

The process of making laws is demanding for everyone who is involved. Good ideas compete with other good ideas. Good ideas compete with questionable ideas. Priorities compete for the top spot. Budgets are limited. Evidence and perspectives conflict with other evidence and other perspectives as presentations are made to legislative committees. Votes must be taken. Decisions must be made.

The political process involves compromise; yet, the attainment of bestness requires that what matters most and what works best will be done. Political compromise and pursuit of bestness can work together from a common foundation of (A) classroom reality and (B) dedication to doing what matters most and doing what works best. Once the classroom reality is fully known, the proper actions to take and the improper actions to avoid will become clear. This helps avoid a compromise which is merely the merging of two ideas resulting in a hybrid which is not ideal and which may be impractical to implement.

In the creation of laws, regulations, and policies about education, compromise is more a part of the process than it is of the actual end result. Compromise need not mean taking parts of two incompatible ideas and combining them so something can get approved. Compromise should mean setting aside any objective other than bestness.

With agreement on that objective, the spirit of compromise leads to a process of cooperation.

EPILOGUE

When asked "what has changed in education during the years you have been a teacher," an experienced educator may express concerns plus successes and insights. Concerns could include the following:

(1) Among some children and some teenagers, excessive cell phone use to the point of addiction consumes far too much time daily. That is time not spent on school work.

(2) Among children and teenagers who imitate ubiquitous popular culture – television, movies, music, video games, social media and more – the result is a decline in proper behavior plus a reduction of commitment to and time for school work.

(3) Among a growing number of students, perhaps high school students especially, the reluctance or refusal to read and to do other school work is creating intellectual deficiencies.

(4) The part-time jobs some high school students have with 20, 25, or 30 hours weekly can have a negative impact on school attendance and on effort made at

school.

Successes and insights could include the following:

(1) Some of today's highest achieving students are doing academic work that is as good or is better than prior high-achieving students did.
(2) What great teachers have always done continues to work.
(3) Teaching is more complex, more complicated, and more tiring or fatiguing than ever. Learning to take good care of themselves is vital for teachers. Working 50-60 productive hours weekly is better than working 60-75 exhausted hours.
(4) The purpose of a school is to cause learning. The bottom line is: was learning caused?
(5) Every decision, every action at a school and in the education bureaucracy or hierarchy should be consistent with doing only what matters most and what works best to cause learning.

When everything works the way it should at the best school, students learn and teachers get results, which can enable a teacher to write a letter of recommendation such as the following:

To Whom It May Concern:
Letter of Recommendation for Mary Biswell

This letter is sent to strongly recommend that your college or university accept Mary Biswell for admission to begin her college career with the 2017-2018 academic year. Currently, Mary is a senior at Lombardy County High School in Patterson, Kentucky. She will graduate from high school in May 2017. During her junior year of high school, Mary took an Advanced Placement (AP) United States History class which I taught.

Mary did outstanding work in our AP United States History class. She earned a grade of A in each semester of the class. She also scored a five, which is the highest possible score on the AP United States History exam.

Mary was always well-prepared for class and she was always very involved in class. Her work ethic and her eagerness to learn are inspiring. Her contributions to class discussions were scholarly. She showed a college level understanding of the facts and concepts in U.S. History. Her thinking as expressed in written answers on tests was profound. Your professors will be delighted with the intellectual impact Mary has on classes. She will certainly contribute to academic life at your college or university.

You will enjoy getting to know Mary. She has exemplary people skills. She is polite, cordial, appreciative, and respectful. She has many friends at school. She is quite admired by the faculty of this school.

Mary is very active at school and in the community. She has been involved with the Speech and Debate team. She has won several awards for her debating skills. She also was on the school's bowling team and helped them win a state championship. Mary has volunteered for three years at a local community food bank. She also has gone on two summer mission trips with her church youth group. Mary will bring her eagerness to be involved to your college or university. Campus life will benefit from Mary's participation.

With complete confidence, I strongly encourage you to accept Mary Biswell for admission. She is prepared to be a very successful college student.

Sincerely,
Robert Johnson, teacher

There are many students who are conscientious, who behave well, who achieve much, who do what is right, who work, who think, who learn, and who are polite. These students deserve the learning opportunities which will enable them to maximize their abilities so they all become the best student and so they always maintain bestness.

There are some students who have not yet become conscientious. There are some students who have not yet mastered the skills and the disciplines of consistently doing what is right, of consistently working and thinking and learning, and of consistently being polite. Notice, those two sentences reflect the essential optimism which educators must maintain. Any student who has not yet reached the desired levels of academic achievement and/or of proper behavior is a unique work in progress who the educators at the best school are determined to continue working with so those students also reach bestness.

There are many meaningful rewards which can be found for people who work in education. The classroom can be a place where students are given vital learning experiences which can help shape their lives in very important and in very proper ways. Being part of that process is to know that the work you do has a vital, lasting importance. Working in the classroom or working in other positions which support what teachers and students do in classrooms is a contribution to people, to life itself, to the human pursuit of bestness and to the attainment of bestness.

School matters. Education matters. Learning matters. Being the best matters. Making contributions to those academic endeavors which matter can add much meaning and value to a life well lived. Working at the best school is demanding and is worth it. Persist. Be the best.

ACKNOWLEDGMENTS

Thank you to Adam Turner, founder of Cherrymoon Media. Adam's support for this book has been essential. His talents in transforming a manuscript into a book are superior.

Thank you to Bob, Laura, Robert, Julie, and Brian. My brother, sister-in-law, nephews and niece encourage and guide me. I cherish them.

Thank you to my parents and to my grandparents – Bob and Judy Babbage, Keen and Eunice Johnson. I miss them deeply, yet I am eternally thankful for them and inspired by them. They highly valued education. They made sure I was a conscientious student. They supported and encouraged my career in education.

Thanks to the educators and the students I have worked with throughout my career. We have accomplished so much together.

ABOUT THE AUTHOR

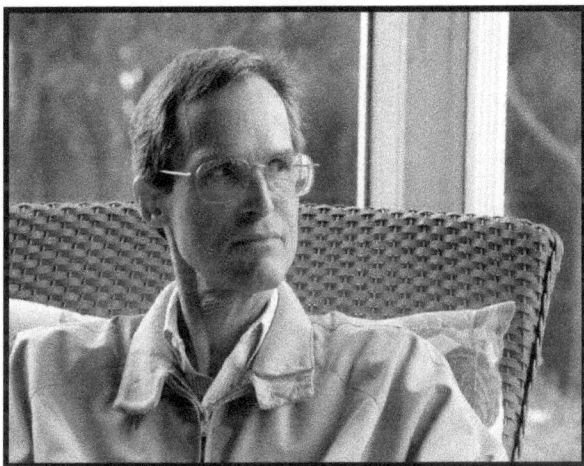

Keen Babbage, Ed. D., retired from a 27-year career in public education in 2016. He had been a middle school teacher, a middle school assistant principal, and a high school teacher. Earlier in his career, he worked for five years at two private schools. He has also worked in advertising/marketing for eight years at three large companies.

He has written 19 other books about education in two areas of emphasis: teaching and school leadership/management. He has written three additional books: *Life Lessons from Cancer* (which was coauthored by Laura Babbage), *Life Lessons from a Dog Named Rudy*, and *Take More Naps*. He currently resides in Lexington, KY.